Nashua Public Library

Enjoy this book!
Please remember to return it on time
so that others may enjoy it too.

Manage your library account and
discover all we offer by visiting us
online at www.nashualibrary.org

Love your library? Tell a friend!

J

Invasive Species Takeover

NORTHERN SNAKE HEADS

BARBARA CILETTI

BLACK
RABBIT
BOOKS

Bolt is published by Black Rabbit Books
P.O. Box 3263, Mankato, Minnesota, 56002.
www.blackrabbitbooks.com
Copyright © 2017 Black Rabbit Books

Design and Production by Michael Sellner
Photo Research by Rhonda Milbrett

Library of Congress Control Number: 2015954689

HC ISBN: 978-1-68072-016-7   PB ISBN: 978-1-68072-280-2

Printed in the United States at CG Book Printers,
North Mankato, Minnesota, 56003. PO #1793 4/16

Web addresses included in this book were working and appropriate at the time of publication. The publisher is not responsible for broken or changed links.

Image Credits
Flickr: Adam H. Field, 28 (middle); Daniel A. Reidel, 3, 20; iStock: mansum008, 15; SafakOguz, 22–23; Newscom: RICHARD B. LEVINE, 24; Ontario Ministry of Natural Resources and Forestry: Nick Lapointe, 10 (fish); opencage.info: 13; Photo Courtesy of Morgan Kupfer of Tight Lined Tales of a Fly Fisherman: 14; Science Source: 6–7; Shutterstock: chungking, 28 (top), 31; Ficmajstr, 19 (bottom); Formosan-Fish, Cover, 4–5; La Gorda, 22, 23; macknimal, 19 (top); Peter Hermes Furian, 10–11 (map); StockPhotoAstur, 18; wawritto, 22, 23; zcw, 8–9; tnaqua.org: Photo by Todd Stailey, Tennessee Aquarium ©2016, 28 (bottom), 32; Wikimedia: Brian Gratwicke, Back Cover, 1, 13, 27
Every effort has been made to contact copyright holders for material reproduced in this book. Any omissions will be rectified in subsequent printings if notice is given to the publisher.

Contents

CHAPTER 1

A Surprising

One day, a man was fishing in the Potomac River. Suddenly, his rod nearly bent in half! He tugged and struggled. Finally, he pulled a fish from the water. But the fish wasn't the kind he expected.

A Snake Fish?

The man had never seen a fish like that before. It had the head of a snake and a long, round body. It was 3 feet (1 meter) long. And it weighed more than 17 pounds (8 kilograms). He had caught a northern snakehead.

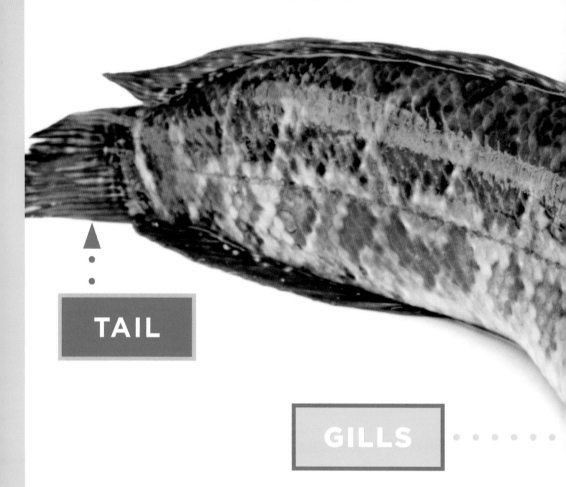

TAIL

GILLS

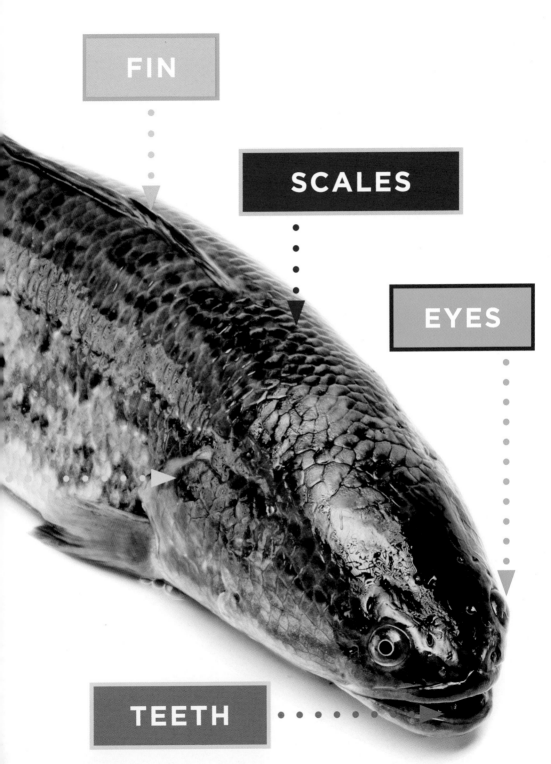

FIN

SCALES

EYES

TEETH

Invasive Species

Snakeheads are not supposed to be in the Potomac River. Several years ago, people brought the fish into the United States. The fish easily spread from one river or lake to another. They hurt the animals that already lived there. Snakeheads are an **invasive species**.

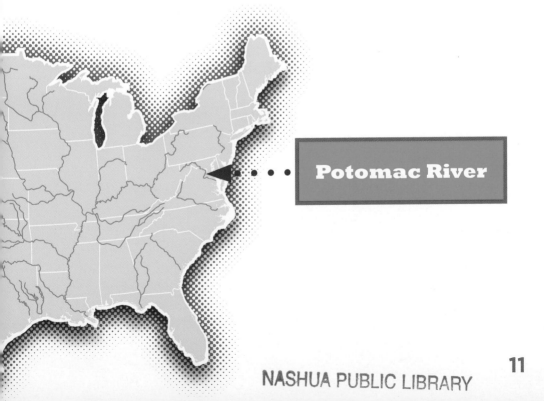

Potomac River

CHAPTER 2

Spreading Out

Snakeheads are from China, Russia, and Korea. They live in freshwater ponds, rivers, and **marshes**. Some people brought snakeheads to sell in U.S. fish markets. Others kept the fish as pets. People eventually dropped unwanted snakeheads into U.S. rivers.

Live Snakeheads Brought to the United States

373
1997

1,488
1998

6,044
1999

8,650
2000

18,991
2001

15,688
2002

On the Move

The snakeheads began laying eggs in their new homes. Females lay up to 100,000 eggs a year. The baby fish grow quickly. Young snakeheads then spread to other water areas. They even wiggle across areas of land to get to other bodies of water.

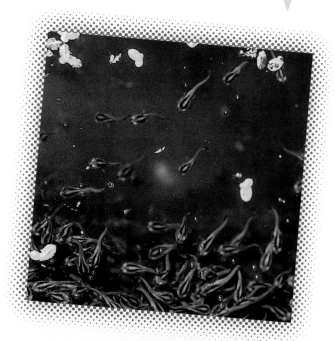

NORTHERN SNAKEHEADS

Canada

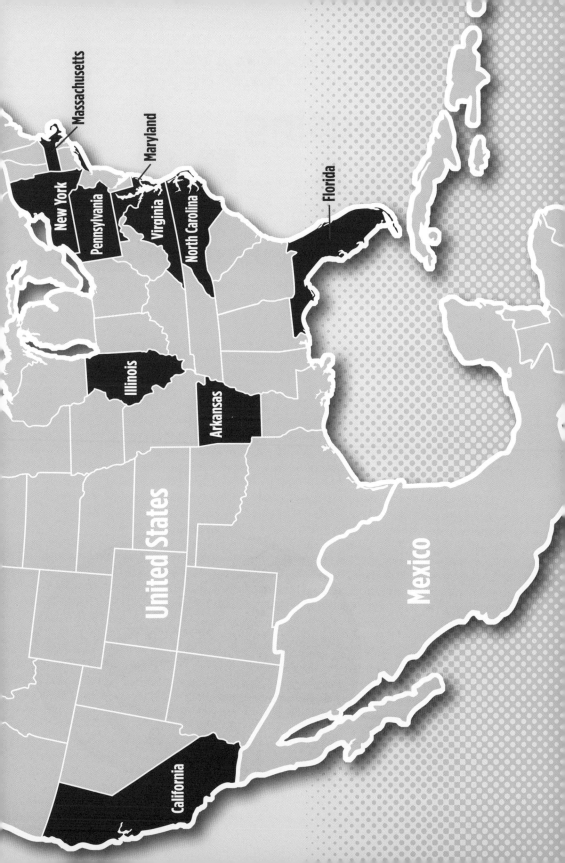

Massachusetts

Maryland

Florida

New York

Pennsylvania

Virginia

North Carolina

Illinois

Arkansas

United States

Mexico

California

CHAPTER 3

Causing

Northern snakeheads cause trouble for other water animals. Snakeheads eat reptiles, birds, mammals, and other fish. They eat the food other animals need. Other fish starve to death.

small birds

What Snakeheads Eat

other fish

frogs

Take Over

Snakeheads are top **predators**. Very few things eat snakeheads. So their populations continue to grow. Scientists worry that snakeheads will kill **endangered** animals. They also worry that snakeheads will harm water **ecosystems**.

FISH IN THE POTOMAC RIVER

NORTHERN SNAKEHEAD

average length: more than 2–3 feet
(61–85 centimeters)

PIKE

average length: 2.3–3.9 feet
(70-119 cm)

STRIPED BASS
average length: 2.2–3.3 feet
(67–101 cm)

SPOTTED SEA TROUT
average length: 1.6–2.1 feet
(49–64 cm)

SPANISH MACKEREL
average length: 1.2–1.5 feet
(37–46 cm)

SUMMER FLOUNDER
average length:
1.3–1.7 feet
(40–52 cm)

IF YOU CATCH THIS FISH, DO NOT RELEASE.
IT IS HIGHLY INVASIVE AND A THREAT TO THE ECOSYSTEM.

New York State Department of Environmental Conservation

- Be sure to secure the fish so that it does not re-enter the Harlem Meer.
- Please keep in a secure container until it is picked up by officials.
- Please bring it immediately to Central Park Conservancy staff located at the Dana Center.
- If the Dana Center is closed, please call 311 and report the capture of a northern snakehead

CENTRAL PARK
CONSERVANCY
central to the park

24

CHAPTER 4

Stopping Snakeheads

Scientists are working to stop the spread of snakeheads. Lawmakers made it illegal to bring snakeheads to the United States. But some people break the law.

People have used **chemicals** to kill snakeheads. But these chemicals also kill other animals. Scientists are trying to find other ways to get rid of snakeheads.

Trouble

Snakeheads are a big problem in some places. If not stopped, they could cause other animals to die out. That's why these invaders must be stopped.

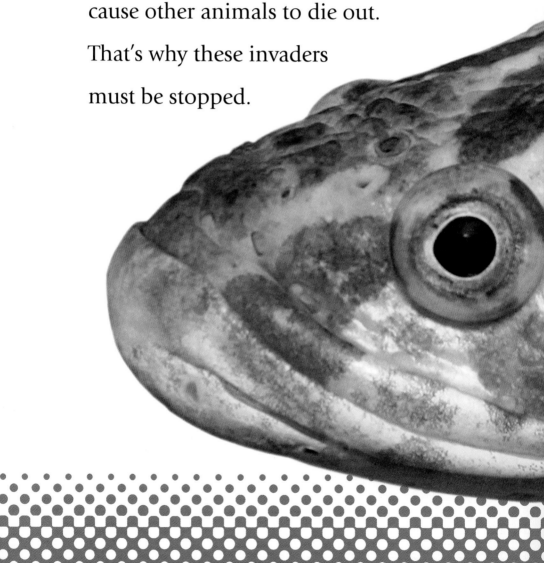

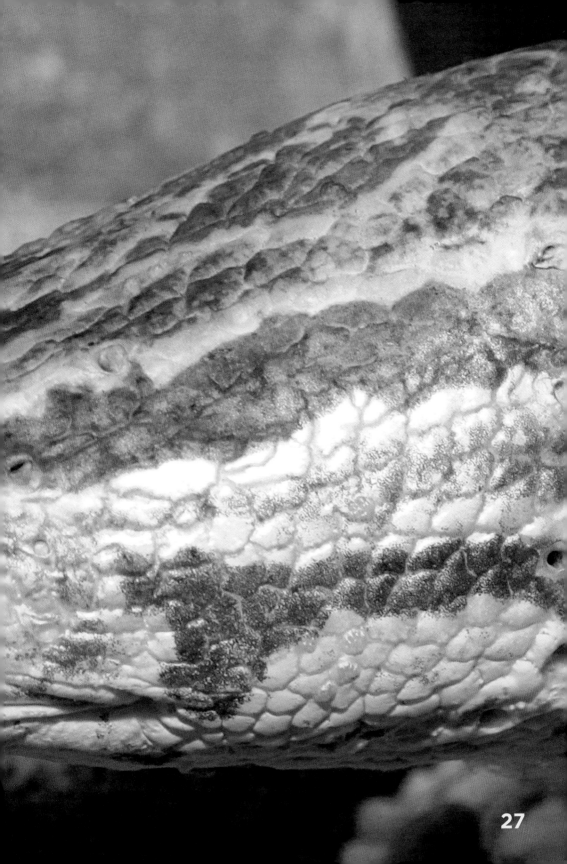

NORTHERN SNAKEHEADS BY THE NUMBERS

15 to 18 pounds
(7 to 8 kilograms)

average weight

24 to 48 HOURS

time it takes for eggs to hatch

4 DAYS
time a snakehead can survive out of water

6 FEET
(2 meters)

length of longest snakehead ever found

28

Think about It...

1. Chemicals kill snakeheads. But many people don't want to use them. Use other sources to find out why chemicals might not be a good solution.

2. What do you think should be done about snakeheads? Use facts to support your answer.

3. The text says that scientists "worry that snakeheads will harm water ecosystems." Use other sources to find out why they are worried.

chemical (KE-muh-kuhl)—a substance that can cause a change in other substance

ecosystem (E-co-sys-tum)—a community of living things in one place

endangered (in-DAYN-jurd)—close to becoming extinct

gill (GYL)—an organ in fish used to get oxygen from water

invasive species (in-VAY-siv SPEE-seez)—animals or plants that spread through an area where they are not native, often causing problems for native plants and animals

marsh (MARSH)—an area of soft wetland that usually has grasses and cattails

predator (PRED-uh-tuhr)—an animal that eats other animals

LEARN MORE

Kallio, Jamie. *12 Things to Know about Invasive Species.* Today's News. Mankato, MN: Peterson Pub. Co., 2015.

O'Connor, Karen. *The Threat of Invasive Species.* Animal 911: Environmental Threats. New York: Gareth Stevens Publishing, 2014.

Spilsbury, Richard. *Invasive Species Underwater.* Invaders from Earth. New York: PowerKids Press, 2015.

WEBSITES

Northern Snakehead
www.chesapeakebay.net/fieldguide/critter/ northern_snakehead

Northern Snakehead
www.fishwild.vt.edu/snakeheads/Facts.html

Northern Snakehead
www.nyis.info/index.php?action=invasive_ detail&id=56

INDEX